An I Can Read Book™

Amazing WHALES!

Written by Sarah L. Thomson

Photographs provided by the
Wildlife Conservation Society

HarperCollins*Publishers*

WILDLIFE CONSERVATION SOCIETY

A blue whale is as long

as a basketball court.

Its eyes are as big as softballs.

Its tongue weighs as much

as an elephant.

It is the biggest animal
that has ever lived on Earth—
bigger than any dinosaur.

But not all whales are this big.

A killer whale is about as long

as a fire truck.

Dolphins and porpoises

are whales too,

very small whales.

The smallest dolphin

is only five feet long.

That's probably shorter

than your mom.

There are about 80 kinds of whales.

All of them are mammals.

Dogs and monkeys and people
are mammals, too.

They are warm-blooded.

This means that their blood
stays at the same temperature
even if the air or water
around them
gets hot or cold.

Mammal babies drink milk
from their mothers.
Whale babies are called calves.

And mammals breathe air.
A whale must swim
to the ocean's surface to breathe
or it will drown.
After a whale calf is born,
its mother may lift it up
for its first breath of air.

A whale uses its blowholes
to breathe.

It can have one blowhole or two.

The blowholes are on the top
of its head.

When a whale breathes out,
the warm breath
makes a cloud called a blow.

Then the whale breathes in.

Its blowholes squeeze shut.

The whale dives under the water.

It holds its breath
until it comes back up.

When sperm whales hunt,

they dive deeper

than any other whale.

They can hold their breath

for longer than an hour

and dive down more than a mile.

Deep in the ocean,
where the water is
dark and cold,
sperm whales hunt
for giant squid
and other animals.

Some whales, like sperm whales,
have teeth to catch their food.
They are called toothed whales.
Other whales have no teeth.
They are called baleen whales.
(Say it like this: bay-LEEN.)
Blue whales and humpback whales
are baleen whales.
They have strips of baleen
in their mouths.
Baleen is made of the same stuff
as your fingernails.
It is strong but it can bend.

15

A baleen whale

fills its mouth with water.

In the water

there might be fish or krill.

Krill are tiny animals like shrimp.

The whale closes its mouth.

The water flows back out

between the strips of baleen.

The fish or krill are trapped

inside its mouth

for the whale to eat.

Some whales, like killer whales,
hunt in groups to catch their food.
These groups are called pods.
A whale mother and her children,
and even her grandchildren,
sometimes live in one pod.

When all the killer whales
in a pod hunt together,
they can kill and eat a whale
that is bigger than they are.

A killer whale calls

to other whales in its pod.

The calls sound like squeaks or whistles.

Other whales make sounds

like groans or chirps or creaks.

Male humpback whales make sounds

over and over, like a song.

Their songs go on for hours

and can be heard for miles.

No one is sure why they sing.

Humpback whales also jump

out of the water

and splash back down.

Some other whales do this, too.

It is called breaching.

People think

this may be a way

whales signal to other whales.

What do the signals mean?

No one knows for sure.

Whales are the biggest animals
in the world.
But killer whales and sharks
sometimes hunt whales.
And so do people.

24

· Once, there were more
than a hundred thousand
humpback whales.
Now there are probably
around thirty thousand.
One kind of right whale
is in even more trouble—
there are only three hundred left.

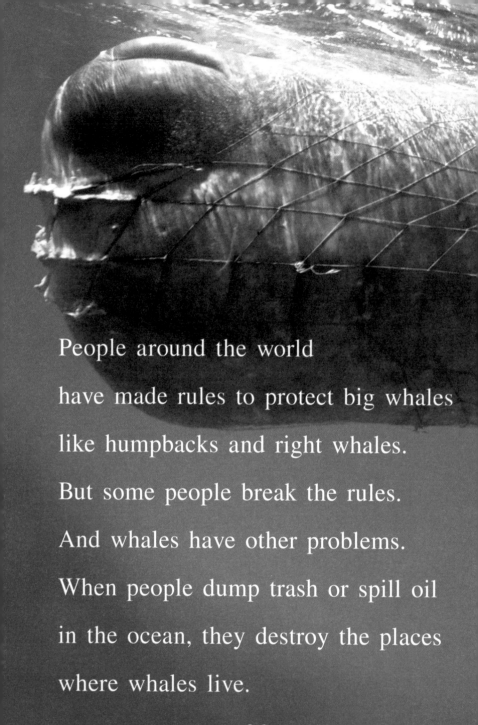

People around the world

have made rules to protect big whales

like humpbacks and right whales.

But some people break the rules.

And whales have other problems.

When people dump trash or spill oil

in the ocean, they destroy the places

where whales live.

Whales also get hit by boats.

They get caught in fishing nets.

If they are not freed, they cannot eat

or swim to the surface to breathe.

Scientists go out in boats

to count how many whales

are still alive.

They also follow whales and listen

to the sounds that whales make.

They ask questions like:

Are the whales in a pod one family?

Do they signal to each other?

Do they stay in one place

or swim for many miles?

Everything scientists find out will

help us keep whales safe.

New rules help us to protect whales.

The number of humpbacks has grown.

But many whales are still in danger.

All whales need help to survive.

People can keep the ocean clean.

We can make safe places

where whales will not be hunted

or hurt by boats or nets.

With our help,

whales will swim in the ocean

for a long time to come.

The Wildlife Conservation Society and Whales

The Wildlife Conservation Society (WCS) saves wildlife and wild lands around the world, studies and teaches about what animals need to survive, and runs the world's largest system of zoos, including the Bronx Zoo in New York City.

Since whales spend most of their lives underwater, they are difficult to study. Scientists must go out in boats to learn how whales live in the wild. Everything that scientists learn about whales helps organizations like WCS understand the best ways to help them. WCS works with governments in many countries to set up places where whales will be safe. WCS scientist Dr. Howard Rosenbaum and his team have made special studies of whale populations around the world. Their work with humpback whales in two African nations, Madagascar and Gabon, has helped to protect some of the places near shore where humpback calves are born.

To find out more about WCS and the ways that you can help whales and other endangered animals, visit www.wcs.org.

With gratitude to Peter Hamilton.
Special thanks to Dr. Howard Rosenbaum, WCS scientist, whale expert, and consultant. Thanks for photographs to Brandon Cole (jacket front, front flap, pages 4-5, 6-7, 8, 12-13, 14, 16-17, 18-19, 20-21, 23, 24-25, 32) as well as Doc White (pages 2-3), François Gohier (page 11), Dennis DeMello (page 9), Yvette Razafindrakoto, WCS/AMNH CRCP (title page), Eleanor Sterling, WCS/AMNH CRCP (pages 28-29), Peter J. Ersts, WCS/AMNH CRCP (pages 30-31), and Kike Calvo/V&W/Seapics (pages 26-27).

HarperCollins®, 🐳®, and I Can Read Book® are trademarks of HarperCollins Publishers Inc.

Library of Congress Cataloging-in-Publication Data
Thomson, Sarah L. Amazing Whales! / written by Sarah L. Thomson ; photographs provided by the Wildlife Conservation Society.
p. cm. (An I Can Read Book) ISBN-10: 0-06-054465-1 (trade bdg.) — ISBN-10: 0-06-054466-X (lib. bdg.) — ISBN-10: 0-06-054467-8 (pbk.) ISBN-13: 978-0-06-054465-2 (trade bdg.) — ISBN-13: 978-0-06-054466-9 (lib. bdg.) — ISBN-13: 978-0-06-054467-6 (pbk.) 1. Whales—Juvenile literature. I. Wildlife Conservation Society (New York, N.Y.) II. Title. III. Series. QL737.C4T45 2004 599.5—dc22 2004002473

❖